Henry Hudson

Ruth Manning

Heinemann Library
Chicago, Illinois

©2001 Reed Educational & Professional Publishing
Published by Heinemann Library,
an imprint of Reed Educational & Professional Publishing,
Chicago, IL

Customer Service 888-454-2279

Visit our website at www.heinemannlibrary.com

Designed by Wilkinson Design
Illustrated by Art
Printed by Wing King Tong, in Hong Kong

05 04 03 02 01
10 9 8 7 6 5 4 3 2 1

Library of Congress Cataloging-in-Publication Data
Manning, Ruth.
  Henry Hudson / Ruth Manning.
    p. cm. – (Groundbreakers)
  Includes bibliographical references and index.
  Summary: A biography of the English explorer and sea captain who explored three
North American waterways later named for him—the Hudson River, Hudson Bay, and Hudson Strait.
  ISBN 1-57572-370-0 (lib. bdg.)   ISBN 1-58810-342-0 (pbk. bdg.)
    1. Hudson, Henry, d. 1611—Juvenile literature. 2. Explorers—America—Biography—Juvenile literature. 3.
Explorers—England—Biography—Juvenile literature. 4. America—Discovery and
exploration—English—Juvenile literature. [1.
Hudson, Henry, d. 1611. 2. Explorers. 3. America—Discovery and exploration—English.] I. Title. II. Series.

E129.H8 F67 2000
910'.92—dc21
[B]   00-029563

Acknowledgments   The publisher would like to thank the following for permission to reproduce photographs:
North Wind Pictures, pp. 4, 17, 21, 25, 26, 28, 31, 34, 38; The Granger Collection, pp. 5, 9, 10, 11 (left), 11 (right), 13, 20, 24, 27, 33, 38; Corbis, pp. 7, 19, 39; Clifton Adams/National Geographic Image Collection, p. 14; Mary Evans Picture Library, pp. 15, 30; Fran Coleman/Animals Animals, p. 16; Stock Montage, pp. 18, 36, 37, 41; Mark Adamic, pp. 22, 23; Cindi & John Reinhardt/C&J Enterprises, p. 32; Hudson Bay Company, Canada/The Bridgeman Art Library, p. 35; Super Stock, p. 40; Len Tantillo, p. 41.

Cover photograph: Stock Montage

Some words are shown in bold, **like this.**
You can find out what they mean by looking in the glossary.

Contents

The Mystery Explorer 4

Riches of Asia 6

Europe in the Fifteenth Century 8

Knowledge of the World 10

Resources for Exploration 12

First Voyage—1607 14

Second Voyage—1608 16

Walruses and Mermaids 18

The Dutch Connection 20

The Half Moon 22

Third Voyage—1609 24

Across the Atlantic to Maine 26

South to Cape Hatteras and Back 28

The Inhabitants of the Hudson River 30

Exploring the Hudson River 32

Fourth Voyage—1610 34

Mutiny 36

Aftermath 38

Hudson's Legacy .40

Maps 42

Timeline 44

More Books to Read 45

Glossary 46

Index 48

Henry Hudson's mystery

For a man who accomplished so much, very little is known about Henry Hudson. Scholars believe that he was born sometime around 1565 and died sometime after June of 1611. Almost nothing is known about his early life. Records show that he had a wife, Katherine, and three sons, Oliver, John, and Richard. John sailed with him as his cabin boy.

There is not a lot of information about Hudson's life, but there are more detailed records of the four great trips he made by sea, looking for a northern route to Asia. The Hudson family was active in the Muscovy Company, which sponsored several of Henry's trips. In 1585 John Davis was staying with Thomas Hudson in London as he planned a trip to hunt for a Northwest Passage from England to Asia. It is possible that Henry met Davis in London, and that Davis is the person who made him curious about Arctic trade routes.

This portrait of Henry Hudson by Paul Van Somer dates to 1620.

We do not know where Henry Hudson went to school, or where he learned to sail ships. He must have been a skilled **navigator** for two important trading companies to entrust him with ships for the difficult task of leading an expedition by sea in the cold, snow, ice, fog, and currents of Arctic waters.

Four great voyages of exploration

Hudson sailed three times for the English and once for the Dutch. On his first two voyages, he headed north looking for a route to Asia. In 1607, he was turned back at Spitzbergen by the polar ice pack after sailing close to the coast of Greenland. In 1608, he took a more easterly direction going around the top of the Scandinavian peninsula and on to islands off the coast of Russia and Siberia before the ice forced him to return.

In 1609 Hudson sailed under the direction of a Dutch company, and explored the east coast of North America from Nova Scotia, Canada, down past the Chesapeake Bay to North and South Carolina. He sailed into Delaware Bay and up the Hudson River. His last journey, in 1610, was for an English company. This time his route went around Iceland and Greenland, then into Hudson Bay in what is now Canada.

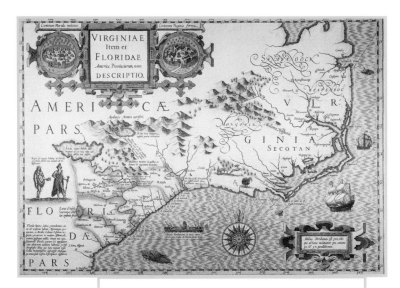

This 1606 map by Jodocus Hondius shows the American southeast from St. Augustine, Florida to the Chesapeake Bay.

Although Henry Hudson failed to find a northern route to Asia, he added to our knowledge of **uncharted** territory. Hudson Bay, Hudson River, and Hudson **Straits** are named after him.

FACTS

Sailing without good maps
Sailors exploring new territory had to depend on good luck and a lot of guesswork. There was no way of knowing which river or bay might lead to a shipping route to Asia. Henry Hudson's trip up the Hudson River, though important because of the new land explored, was just another in a long line of failed attempts to reach Asia.

Riches of Asia

Silks and spices

Hudson was hired to find a fast and easy sea route to Asia because the British and Dutch merchants needed a cheaper and faster way to get spices, fabrics, and ceramics to sell in Europe. Over 2,000 years ago, the Greeks and Romans knew of the wonders of products from the east because of a long series of trade routes, known as the **Silk Road,** that stretched from China to the shores of the Mediterranean Sea. The Silk Road was not a single road, but a number of paths, some over water, but most over land. Most of its length covered very rough **terrain**. The length was over 4,000 miles (6,400 kilometers), but most traders did not go the full distance. They bought and sold goods over a small segment of the road.

Over the Silk Road passed corals, pearls, amber, glass, and woven cloth from the countries of the Mediterranean. From Asia came spices such as cinnamon from the spice islands of the East Indies, lacquerware, and especially silk from China. Soldiers from England and northern Europe traveled east in the twelfth and thirteenth centuries in order to win back the Holy Land from the **Muslims,** in wars called the Crusades. In the Middle East, they discovered products from Asia that they wanted back home.

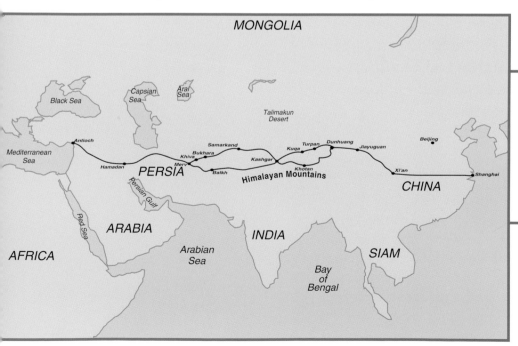

Silk that was made in China would be handled by many traders over the Silk Road before it reached the markets of Mediterranean countries.

The traders

With the demand for goods created by the Crusades, trade developed in England and the countries of northern Europe. However, products from Asia cost a great deal in transportation and middlemen's fees. It is usually much cheaper and faster to send goods by sea than by land. People started to wonder if there was an easier way to get the goods from Asia to Europe.

Every country wanted to be the first to find a sea route to Asia. The Portuguese were the first to try. They sent explorers down around Africa and into the Indian Ocean at the end of the fifteenth century and the beginning of the sixteenth century. This made the northern countries curious—could there be a route to the north, closer to England and the Netherlands, that would be worth finding and using?

In the twentieth century, people were still wondering whether they could find a good Arctic sea route. They wanted a fast way to go from the Alaska oil fields to the east coast of the United States. The first commercial vessel to make its way through the Northwest Passage—up through the Arctic over Canada—was the *Manhattan* in 1969. It carried a single barrel of oil as a symbol of the trade possible by this route. The *Manhattan* had to be fitted with special equipment for breaking through ice. Stan Haas, the manager of this $43 million expedition, is reported to have said: "If the Northwest Passage does become operable, the whole world could benefit."

Only in 1969 did the first commercial vessel make its way through the Northwest Passage from Alaska to New York. The ice tore a bus-sized hole in the unarmored cargo tank and cracked the hull of the Manhattan.

Europe in the Fifteenth Century

Portugal and Spain

By the time Hudson left on his first voyage in 1607, two sea routes to Asia had already been found. In 1497–99, Vasco da Gama, a Portuguese explorer, succeeded in traveling all the way to India by sea. His voyage sailed around the southern tip of Africa, which he named the Cape of Good Hope. This opened up new trade opportunities for Portugal.

Christopher Columbus, sailing from Spain, set out to find India by sailing west in 1492. His return with news of gold and new lands to the west triggered a rush on the part of Spanish soldiers, the **conquistadors,** to explore and settle the new territories. The new world had rich mines of gold that the conquistadors sent back to the king in Spain. This gold was used to fund wars that the Spaniards were fighting for their **empire** in Europe.

The Portuguese and the Spanish rulers were also disagreeing over which empire owned the land in the New World. They looked to the **pope** to divide the new territories between them. A papal declaration of 1493 was modified by a treaty of 1494. When the struggle for land had stopped, the Spanish could continue to explore routes to Asia. In 1519–1522, Ferdinand Magellan was the first person to circle the world and establish a southwest route to Asia.

The 1494 treaty between Portugal and Spain divided the territories in the New World. South America is now made up of independent countries, but the countries that used to belong to Spain still speak Spanish, and the ones Portugal owned still speak Portuguese.

England and the Netherlands

There were enormous changes in the way people lived during the fifteenth and sixteenth centuries. In religion, the pope's authority came under attack as **Reformation** ideas swept over Europe. Henry VIII divorced his Spanish wife, Catherine, breaking away from the Roman Catholic Church. The ideas of John Calvin, a religious reformer, influenced the population of what was to become the Netherlands to revolt against Spain.

At the beginning of the sixteenth century, the territory of the Netherlands belonged to Spain and was part of the empire ruled by the Spanish king. But when Spain tried to put down the actions and ideas of Reformation leaders in the Netherlands, it led to revolt and the formation of the Republic. The Eighty-Years' War, from 1568 to 1648, found the English helping the fighters for the new Dutch Republic.

The British Navy was not expected to defeat the Spanish Armada, which was considered by many to be unbeatable. However, the weather played a large part in their victory.

The English had become more powerful under Queen Elizabeth I, whose navy had defeated the fleet of ships called the **Spanish Armada.** English expeditions and pirates set sail to lay claim to some of the gold and land of the New World. This brought an increase of population and wealth to England. Elizabeth was followed on the throne by James I in 1603.

Prior expeditions

Portugal and Spain had a head start in exploring the New World, but the rest of the European countries soon sent out explorers, too. In 1497, England sent John Cabot to find a route to the Indies. He discovered Newfoundland, now part of Canada, and claimed the land for England. In 1508, John's son Sebastian sailed south along the east coast to North Carolina, or perhaps even Florida, looking for a sea route to Asia.

It was Jacques Cartier who first explored the Gulf of Saint Lawrence as he looked for a northwest passage to Asia.

Around 1524, Giovanni da Verrazano, backed by French silk merchants and bankers from Italy, sailed under the French flag from someplace south of North Carolina up to the Arctic with a stop in New York Harbor. On a later voyage he was eaten by cannibals in the West Indies.

From 1534 to 1541, Jacques Cartier made three voyages for France and discovered that the Gulf of St. Lawrence was not the Northwest Passage to Asia. Martin Frobisher of England made three voyages from 1576 to 1578. Finding snow in July convinced him that winter would be extreme in Labrador, Baffin Bay, and the Hudson **Straits.** Finally, John Davis made three trips between 1585 and 1587, exploring Greenland and traveling into Baffin Bay as far as the ice would permit. He was convinced that this was the way to Asia.

Maps

We know now that the Vikings and possibly even other explorers had reached the coast of North America from Europe around 1000 A.D., but Hudson and other explorers in the sixteenth century did not know this. While the explorers that went before Hudson gave reports of value about the land and conditions they found, they were not able to provide the kind of maps that we have now.

While **latitude**—the distance from the equator—could be estimated with the instruments available, there was no reliable way of measuring **longitude**—the distance east or west on the earth's surface. The concept was known, but the only measurement was by a comparison of the local time with the time at a fixed point. An accurate **chronometer** to perform this measurement had not yet been invented and would not be available until the eighteenth century.

Henry Hudson would have been trained in current navigation techniques, learning how to use the sun and the stars to find his position. At the time he sailed, there were many things that sixteenth-century **navigators** had not yet learned to do, so maps of the period were inaccurate.

"Shooting the sun" is what the English called measuring the altitude of the sun from the horizon in the sixteenth century. This was done to fix the latitude in which the ship was sailing. The more accurate and compact quadrant was not invented until 1730.

Resources for Exploration

The English experience

"The shortest route, the northern, has been reserved by Divine Providence for England." These words were written by Roger Barlow in his *Briefe Summe of Geographie,* written in 1540–41. Forty years later, William Bourne analyzed the problem of finding a route to Asia. He came up with five options: a northern route directly over the North Pole, a northeast route through the Kara Sea north of Russia and Asia, a northwest route by way of a **strait** in the Canadian Arctic, a southeast route around the southern end of Africa, and a southwest route around the tip of South America.

Since England was in the northern section of Europe, Bourne's first three options would mean a shorter route. One of England's chief products was warm woollen cloth. An Arctic sea route would make trade with the cold northern countries more profitable, since ships would not have to sail so far to the south. The last two of Bourne's choices could bring the ships into conflict with Spain and Portugal.

When a map places England near the center, it is easy to see why northern trade routes would be more profitable for English merchants.

The Muscovy Company

Sebastian Cabot could find no support in England for his ideas to seek a Northwest Passage, so he went to Spain. There, he was given an important position in the Spanish navigational school and center for its expeditions.

When Cabot returned to England in 1548, he was able to convince 100 merchants in London to support his ideas for exploring routes to the north. With Sebastian Cabot as governor, the company of Merchant Adventurers was formed. This organization, known as the Muscovy Company, **outfitted** three ships "for the search and discovery of the northern part of the world, to open a way and passage to our men for travel to new and unknown kingdoms." The first voyage was led by Sir Hugh Willoughby. He and the crew of two of the ships died when the ships were frozen in the ice. The third ship, captained by Stephen Burrough, reached the town of Arkhangelsk on the Russian coast of the White Sea. The pilot-major, Richard Chancellar, went to Moscow and arranged for trade with Russia. In 1556, ice blocked a second attempt. It was fifty years before the company decided to support Henry Hudson on another attempt to find an Arctic sea route in 1607.

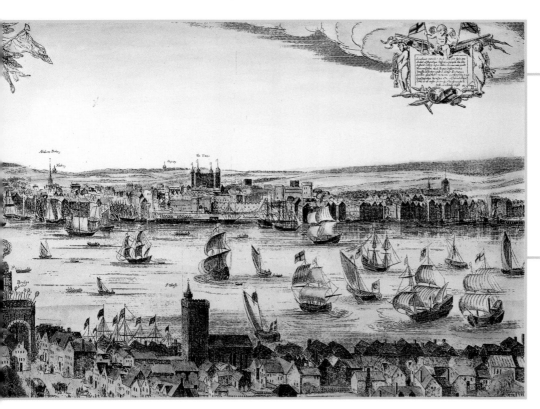

In 1588, London was the largest city in northern Europe. Ships carrying goods from all over the world stopped here.

The route to the North Pole

We know about Hudson's first voyage because of a record written partly by one of the sailors and partly by Hudson. It was found in a book published in 1625. It begins by listing the names of twelve sailors who took **communion** at the Church of Saint Ethelburga in London on April 19, 1607, in preparation of their sailing on May 1. The purpose of their voyage, in the ship called the *Hope-well,* was to discover a passage to Asia by way of the North Pole.

YOU CAN FOLLOW HUDSON'S VOYAGE ON THE MAP ON PAGE 42.

By May 26, the ship had arrived at the Shetland Islands, north of Scotland. Then they turned to the northwest and sighted Greenland on June 13. Here they named a headland, "Young's Cape;" a high mound, "Mount of God's Mercy;" and a portion of the land, "Hold with Hope."

From Greenland they sailed northeast and arrived at Spitzbergen, an island north of Scandinavia, on June 27. They explored this area looking for a path not blocked by ice, but when they couldn't find one Hudson gave the command to turn back to England on July 31. They docked in the Thames River on September 15, 1607.

The old Church of St. Ethelburga in London—where Hudson took communion before his first trip—is the site of this modern 15 foot (4.5 meter) memorial window by Leonard Walker of Rhode Island.

Ice, cold, and fog

We don't know much about life aboard Hudson's ship. The report of the voyage that has come down to us focuses mostly on the sailing conditions, the color of the sea, the bays and inlets, the land and mountains, and the animals the crew encountered. Because they were so far north, the crew observed that the sun did not completely set at night. This phenomenon is known as the "midnight sun."

The danger Hudson's sailors faced does come through in their reports. On July 4, when farther south it was quite hot, Hudson's men report that it was so cold that their sails froze. July 27 was foggy and rainy. The sailors could hear waves breaking on the ice. The sea was pushing them westward toward it. They lowered a small rowboat and tried to tow the *Hopewell* away from danger. However, the seas were so high that they were unsuccessful. Luckily, a northwest-by-west wind—a wind not commonly found on this voyage—came up and blew them away from the ice.

A large part of Spitzbergen is covered by glaciers. The island now belongs to Norway.

FACTS

Icebergs and pack ice
Icebergs and pack ice are a hazard to shipping even today. If an iceberg could sink a modern ship like the *Titanic,* just think how much more damage it could do to the wooden ships of Hudson's day. Icebergs form in spring and summer when the warm weather causes the ice at the edge of glaciers to **calve** and float free. About 10,000 icebergs form each year from the West Greenland glaciers and an average of 375 float south of Newfoundland into the shipping lanes of the North Atlantic.

Search for a northeast passage

The next year—on April 22, 1608—Hudson set out in the *Hope-well* with a crew of fifteen sponsored by the same Muscovy Company. Of the crew, only John Cooke and his son had been on the first voyage. This time Hudson headed north and then east to explore two routes to the Kara Sea—through the sea that is north of Novaya Zemlya, a long narrow island—or by a **strait** or river through that land. Then he thought that he would be able to sail along the coast of Siberia until he reached the Pacific.

There were all sorts of rumors about the warm water beyond the River Ob, which fed into the Kara Sea. A tusk found there was said to be the horn of a unicorn—a mythical animal thought to live in China. Maps of the period were misleading.

Within a month after their departure, Hudson's crew were back in intense cold. Three or four of them were sick. By June 9, they were in ice **floes** so thick and firm that they had to turn the ship around and find their way out for 12 or 15 miles (20 to 25 kilometers), "suffering only a few rubs of our ship against the ice." Again on June 22 they were surrounded by ice. On July 2, they had to fight the ice. At 6:00 A.M. they saw ice from the south floating toward them.

YOU CAN FOLLOW HUDSON'S VOYAGE ON THE MAP ON PAGE 42.

When Hudson explored Novaya Zemlya, its only inhabitants were reindeer and other animals.

More cold and ice

Hudson reported: "We were moored with two anchors ahead, and by letting out one cable, and hauling in the other, we were able to fend off the ice with beams and **spars;** this labor continued until six o'clock in the evening, then it passed us and we rode quietly, having a restful night."

Hudson and his crew explored several rivers to see whether they might offer an arctic route, but found that they were too shallow to sail. The crew that went ashore on Novaya Zemlya came back with birds and eggs. By July 5, Hudson concluded that there was too much ice, and he would not find an arctic passage on this route.

As on the first voyage, ice forced the ship back. Apparently, Hudson then turned his ship to explore to the northwest, but historians believe that the crew had other ideas. On August 7, 1608, Hudson wrote in his log book that he gave his crew a handwritten **certificate** of his free and willing decision to return to England. The certificate stated that the crew had not used force to get

The men of Willem Barent's 1596 expedition built a winter shelter on the island of Novaya Zemlya when their ship was trapped in the ice.

this decision. Why would the certificate have been necessary if there had not been thoughts of **mutiny?** The ship returned to London on August 26, 1608.

Walruses and Mermaids

Animal riches

Hudson did not bring gold back to his merchant sponsors, but he did tell them of the large numbers of whales around Spitzbergen and walruses around Novaya Zemlya. When possible, Hudson's crew had tried to kill walruses, which were valuable for their ivory tusks, their hides, and their **blubber.** Blubber could be made into lamp oil. The crew was not very successful in hunting these animals, but the Muscovy Company would put this information to good use in later years in professional whaling, hunting, and fishing operations.

The animals the Arctic explorers encountered must have been a fearsome sight. Jacques Cartier, an earlier explorer, described a walrus as "a beast big as an oxen, with two teeth in its mouth like an elephant, who lives in the sea." The great white polar bears were said to be "big as a cow, white as a swan."

Hudson reported hearing the roar of the bears on his 1608 trip. He found incredible numbers of seals. Different kinds of birds were brought back for food. The crew also reported the presence of deer and of small animals.

You can follow Hudson's voyage on the map on page 42.

This 19th-century drawing shows a polar bear trying to escape hunters' gunfire.

FACTS

Arctic animals

Hudson and his crew would have seen polar bears, caribou, wolves, foxes, weasels, hares, and lemmings. Also, birds such as the ptarmigan and the snowy owl lived in the Arctic. However, even familiar animals often looked different than the explorers expected. Their fur was specially colored to help them blend into their snowy surroundings.

Mermaid?

Perhaps the most remarkable sighting by the crew was a **mermaid,** or what the crew thought was a mermaid. Hudson noted in his log on June 15, 1608 that two of the crew, Thomas Hiles and Robert Rayner, reported seeing her. One of the men was looking overboard when he saw the mermaid. He called for the rest of the crew to come and look, but only one came. The mermaid was close to the ship's side, looking up at the men. After a few minutes, a wave turned her over so that they could see her better. They described her as having a body as big as theirs, with breasts like a woman's, long black hair, and white skin. When she dove beneath the water they could see her tail, which they reported was "like the tail of a porpoise, and speckled like a mackerel."

Could the men really have seen a mermaid? Many sailors in those days believed in mermaids. Seventeenth-century maps were illustrated with monsters and sea serpents. Water mammals like the dugong and the manatee, which **suckle** their young above water, may be the source of the mermaid stories found in many sailors' accounts.

The mermaid that Hudson's men reported to have seen may in fact have been a manatee.

The Dutch Connection

Negotiations

Two voyages without success must have cooled the interest of the English company. However, many Dutch merchants also wanted to find a trade route to the north. In 1602, they formed the Dutch East India Company—often called the VOC, after the initials of the company's name in Dutch—to protect trade in the Indian Ocean and help the Dutch in their war of independence from Spain. The charter of this company authorized them to wage war and make peace.

The VOC had a fleet consisting of 40 large ships and many smaller ones, 5,000 sailors, and 600 cannons. The Dutch fought other nations over valuable goods like herring, spices, and whales. The company had also offered a prize of 2,500 **florins** to anyone who could discover a northern passage to Asia. The directors asked Hudson to come to Amsterdam, in the Netherlands, for a conference.

Hudson, like many other explorers including Christopher Columbus, was willing to sail under the flag of a country other than his own, as long as that country was willing to finance his trip. The VOC directors did not make their final decision to hire Hudson until they learned that he was also talking with the French about sailing for them.

Dutch merchants of the early seventeenth century carried on trade throughout the world. The profits enabled them to hire artists, such as Rembrandt, to paint them.

This hand-colored woodcut from 1605 shows how Hudson's ships would have looked.

The contract

Henry Hudson's contract with the VOC has been preserved and is one of the main sources of information about him. It is from the contract that we learn the names of his family. Hudson received the small sum of 800 **guilders** for his service, and insurance that if he did not return within a year, his wife would receive an additional 200 guilders. Of course, if he found a good passage, he could expect more money.

The contract stated that Hudson was "to search for a passage by the north around the north side of Novaya Zemlya, and shall continue thus along that parallel until he shall be able to sail southward to the **latitude** of 60 degrees." Hudson's thinking at that time was that the Northwest might be more promising than the Northeast, but before he left the VOC changed the contract, adding that Hudson was required "to think of discovering no other route or passage, except the route around the north or northeast, above Novaya Zemlya. . . . If it could not be accomplished at that time, another route would be subject of consideration for another voyage." Hudson did not obey these restrictions.

The Half Moon

Sources of information

At least two replicas have been built of the *Half Moon,* Hudson's ship on his third voyage, and a good deal of research has gone into trying to discover what the ship looked like. No paintings or engravings of the ship exist, and the ship builders of that day did not use blueprints or written plans.

The best sources of information about the design of the ship come from a 1586 manuscript written by an English shipbuilder—Matthew Baker—and a 1629 account by Josephum Furttenbach, which describes a Dutch ship built in 1628. There are illustrations of the craft both in and out of the water. Both sources show a ship with a broad, flat bottom that could carry a large cargo. The Dutch ships were faster than the English ones because they were lighter and narrower.

Historians have also found the construction order of the VOC. The *Half Moon* was to be 70 feet (21 meters) long and 16 feet (5 meters) wide, with a depth in the hold of 8 feet (2.5 meters). The way the sails were arranged is based on the descriptions in the journal of Robert Juet, one of Hudson's crew members. The ship would look small and cramped compared to today's boats.

*This drawing shows the **rig** and sail plan of the* Half Moon.

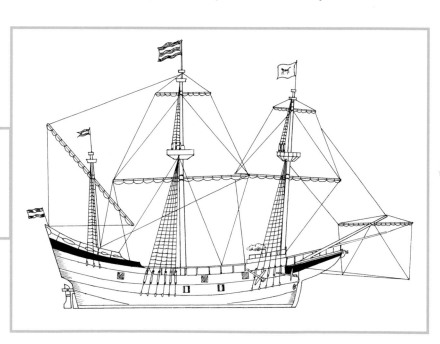

The *Half Moon*'s history

The *Half Moon* was built in Amsterdam in 1608. The VOC directed the building of its ships, using German and Danish lumber and hiring labor to work under its supervision.

The *Half Moon* has a short but interesting history. Henry Hudson set out on his third voyage on this ship from Amsterdam on March 25, 1609 with a crew of sixteen. He returned to Dartmouth, England on November 7, 1609. However, the English prevented Hudson or the English sailors from leaving their country. The *Half Moon* was not returned to the Dutch until after Hudson had set sail on his fourth voyage. This time Hudson was sponsored by English merchants.

In May 1611, the ship—under the command of a Dutch captain—sailed for India. While the fate of the ship is not known for certain, historians believe that the ship was destroyed by the British in fighting around 1618 in the region of Jakarta, in what is now Indonesia.

Two replicas of the ship were later made for celebrations in the United States. In 1909, a copy was built to celebrate the 300-year anniversary of Hudson's third voyage. It was destroyed by a fire in 1934. Another replica was built in 1989 and is based in Croton-on-Hudson, New York.

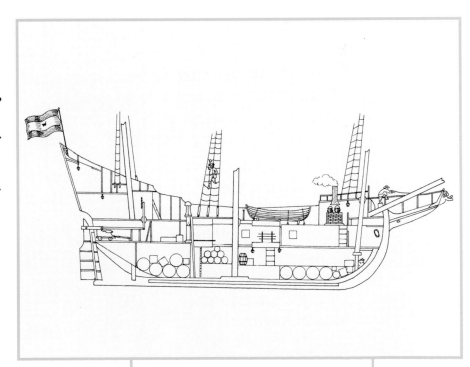

This diagram of the interior shows the use made of the limited space.

Third Voyage—1609

Mutiny?

So how did the *Half Moon*—which was supposed to be on the way to look for a northeast passage—end up sailing to the west? Only a few of Hudson's journal entries have survived. Most of them were sold at public auction in 1821, and no record was kept of the buyers. Historians do have a journal kept by one of the sailors, Robert Juet. His journal was published in 1625.

The ship weighed anchor on March 25, 1609, and sailed up the coast of Norway. However, Hudson and his crew could not get around the North Cape, where they entered the White Sea and encountered storms, "with much wind and snow and very cold." Hudson doubled back, but instead of going back to the Netherlands as his contract required, he sailed west to America.

Did the crew, many of whom were new to the extreme Arctic storms, rebel and refuse to go farther east? Juet does not report what went on as the ship sailed up to the Cape. Was he afraid of writing down his part in what might have been a **mutiny** of sailors who wanted no part of "gusting weather, hail and snow. . . "? In any event, sometime around May 19, 1609, the *Half Moon* turned west and southwest.

YOU CAN FOLLOW HUDSON'S VOYAGE ON THE MAP ON PAGE 42.

The Half Moon *turned around in 1609 and began its journey west to America.*

The southwest coast of England has many ports. This sixteenth-century map shows the protected port of Plymouth.

Spies?

Did Hudson ignore his contract because he secretly was working for the English? In 1612 the Dutch historian Hessel Gerritz wrote that many of the Dutch believed that Hudson "purposely missed the correct route to the western passage, unwilling to benefit Holland and the directors of the Dutch East India Company by such a discovery." Perhaps the Muscovy Company was willing to let the Dutch bear the expense of another search, but planned to claim any discoveries made by the English captain.

Also, how can we explain Hudson sailing back to England at the end of his voyage rather than returning directly to Holland? Was he reporting back to authorities in his own country? It could be that since there were more English than Dutch sailors aboard, a second mutiny had taken place about where to land. Historians have found some evidence for a mutiny in the papers of Emmanuel Van Meteren, the Dutch representative in London with whom Hudson talked and shared his journals. Since Hudson preferred to look for a western rather than an eastern passage, the captain may have used the mutiny as an excuse for sailing 3,000 miles in the wrong direction. In doing so, he had been forced to sail against the prevailing winds, the currents, and the requirements of his contract.

Reaching the New World

By June 1, 1609 the *Half Moon* was out of the range of the midnight sun, which provides light even during night hours. A candle at night was required. The crew tried to find Busse Island, which had been charted by one of the ships of Martin Frobisher in 1578, but they could not find it at the location on the map. No one has since found this island. Perhaps it never existed.

Juet, in his journal, notes the weather, **latitude,** currents, and color of the ocean. On June 15, 1609, he records a great storm that broke one of the **masts** and swept it overboard along with a sail. On June 25, the crew sighted another ship and chased it, but they were not able to catch up or talk to them. July 3 found the ship among a fleet of French vessels that were fishing on the Grand Banks, south of Newfoundland. Juet notes the great number of cod and schools of herring, but says that by July 9, the crew had to limit their catch because they were running out of salt to preserve them. At last on July 12, land was sighted— Cape Sable, Nova Scotia—but instead of going ashore they sailed across the Gulf of Maine.

YOU CAN FOLLOW HUDSON'S VOYAGE ON THE MAP ON PAGE 42.

Dutch ships were a common sight on the seas during the early seventeenth century.

Exploring Maine

The crew prepared to enter the harbor, but the mist was so thick that they could not sail safely among the islands. With the same weather conditions the next day, they had visitors. Juet reports: "At 10 o'clock two boats with six of the savages of the country came out to us, seeming glad of our coming. We gave them trifles and ate and drank with them. They told us there were gold, silver and copper mines close by and that the Frenchmen do trade with them. This is very likely for one of them spoke some words of French."

As soon as they could, the crew anchored in George's Harbor on the St. George River. They went ashore to cut down a tree as a replacement for their mast. They looked for and found fresh water. They also caught 31 lobsters.

More Native Americans came to trade, offering beaver pelts and other furs in exchange for red gowns, knives, hatchets, copper, kettles, beads, and other trinkets that the French often used for barter. The crew was cautious, not knowing what the Indians would do. The Native Americans should have been cautious of the crew, since after they had repaired the mast, they tricked them away from their houses, robbed them, and then set sail to the south.

*Tisquantum, also called Squanto, was captured by English sailors in 1614 but escaped and returned to Massachusetts. When the Pilgrims arrived in 1620 to found the Plymouth **Colony,** he knew some of the English language and was able to teach the newcomers how to plant corn and fertilize it with fish.*

South to Cape Hatteras and Back

Why south?

If Hudson was looking for a northern passage to Asia, why did he sail south? Before Hudson had left Holland, he had received a message from an acquaintance, Captain John Smith of Jamestown, Virginia. Smith believed that there might be a river north of the Virginia **Colony** that could lead to a Western Sea. Perhaps by traveling through the Great Lakes, a person could come to the Pacific Ocean.

The fact that the interior of North America was unexplored led to many surprising theories. The rumors about Lakes Erie, Ontario, Huron, Michigan, and Superior reported that their waters emptied into a large **strait** north of Canada. Also, the maps of the day showed imagination in filling in the blanks of the unknown. Several of them depicted a great sea just behind a narrow strip of land in the middle of the east coast of what is now the United States. Several of these maps also located mythical kingdoms and islands of demons.

YOU CAN FOLLOW HUDSON'S VOYAGE ON THE MAP ON PAGE 42.

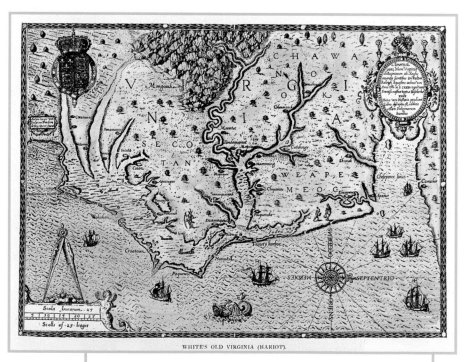

WHITE'S OLD VIRGINIA (HARIOT).

In Hudson's time, it was thought that the James River in Virginia might lead to a water route to China.

The southern route

From Maine, Hudson sailed to Cape Cod. His crew found grapes and rose trees that they brought back to the ship. August 3, 1609 brought them very hot weather. Storms wrecked their **shallop** by ramming it against the **stern** of the ship, so they had to cut the boat loose. They entered the strong Gulf Stream current and were pushed north, but the winds from the north were stronger, and they sailed south.

On August 18, they made an attempt to enter Chesapeake Bay, but a strong northerly wind and rain made them head back to sea. They passed the entrance to the King's River—now called the James River—in Virginia, where they knew that Captain John Smith's colony was located. Why didn't they stop? Even if they did not fly the Dutch flag, their ship was clearly of Dutch design. Perhaps they did not want to be mistaken for enemies of the British.

Storms continued. The ship's cat ran crying from one side of the ship to the other. Since sailors believed that cats had special powers over ships and were related to witches, they were worried by this behavior. Juet reports that on August 24, when the ship was near Cape Hatteras, South Carolina, it turned north. He doesn't explain why. Keeping a record of the inlets they passed, the crew reached the south coast of Staten Island and three great rivers on September 3, 1609.

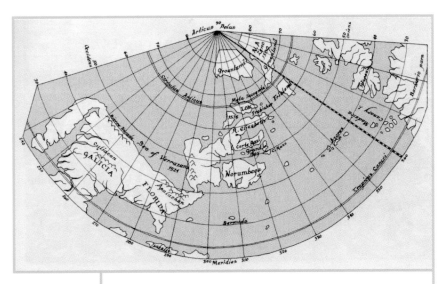

This 1582 map shows the Sea of Verrazano, which Giovanni da Verrazano supposedly discovered in 1524 when he sailed along the outer banks of the Carolinas and saw open water on the far side of a narrow strip of land. He reported that this sea "is the same which flows around the shores of India, China and Cataya...."

The Inhabitants of the Hudson River

Friendly encounters

Henry Hudson left detailed descriptions of the inhabitants of the Hudson River in his journal, which has survived to this day. He reports that when he came on shore, the local residents all gathered around and sang. Their clothes were made of animal skins, mostly foxes, which they had prepared and made into different types of clothing. Their food consisted mostly of baked corn, which Hudson called "Turkish wheat." He reported that "it is excellent eating."

The Native Americans came on board the *Half Moon* one after another, paddling in their canoes, which were made from a single hollowed tree trunk. For weapons they carried bows and arrows, with arrowheads made of sharp stones. Hudson was surprised to note that they had no houses, but "slept under the blue heavens," sometimes on mats made of woven reeds, and sometimes on the leaves of trees. They always carried all their possessions with them, such as their food and strong green tobacco. Hudson concluded that they were a friendly people.

Juet described Indians who gave tobacco to the sailors who went ashore. He said that they dressed in cloaks of feathers and furs and wore copper bands around their necks.

You can follow Hudson's voyage on the map on page 42.

It was common for European explorers to bring trinkets such as beads and mirrors to exchange with Native American tribes. When Hudson met the Mohican Indians, he gave them gifts.

First casualties

Unfortunately, not all encounters with the Native Americans were so friendly. Hudson sent off a **scouting** party of five men in a small boat to test the depth of the river. On their return, the party was attacked by two canoes carrying 26 warriors. One of the sailors, John Colman, was killed by an arrow shot into his throat, and two others were wounded. The scouting party could not find the ship that night and had to row back and forth because the current was so strong that their anchor would not hold them. The place they buried Colman is now known as Colman's Point.

Later, Juet said that one of the Indians stole his pillow and two of his shirts and other items of clothing. The thief was killed.

Another time the ship was attacked by Indians in canoes who fired arrows at the crew. A hundred more waited for them on a point of land. The crew fired six **muskets,** killing two or three tribesmen. Juet set off a light cannon and killed another three. Then the men with the muskets shot three or four more. The Indians retreated to the woods.

C. Smith taketh the King of Pamavnkee prisoner. -1608.

Not all contact with the Native Americans was friendly, as shown in this 1608 engraving of a Jamestown colonist confronting an Indian.

FACTS

Henry Hudson—explorer of Delaware?

Two hundred years after Henry Hudson's exploration of what is now New York, the New York Historical Society decided to hold a celebration to remember his voyage. Since then, Hudson has been associated with New York in the minds of many people. However, the state of Delaware objects to New York claiming Hudson, pointing out that Hudson explored Delaware Bay and the Delaware River before heading north to New York. Hudson had to check out as many rivers and bays as he could to make sure he was not passing up a possible route to Asia.

Exploring the Hudson River

How far inland could they go?

On September 9, 1609, Hudson's crew hoisted anchor and moved into the river channel. They passed the east sandbank of the Narrows and continued on. They saw that the harbor they reached was good protection from the winds. Indians continued to come to the ship to sell items, and the crew bought some oysters and beans.

Hudson noted in his journal that "it is as pleasant a land as one need tread upon." He was pleased to find many kinds of lumber that were suitable for making large vats or **casks** and for shipbuilding. The Indians had copper tobacco pipes, so Hudson guessed that copper might naturally exist there. Based on what the Indians said, he also guessed that iron would be found nearby. However, they did not use it and probably had not yet discovered how to prepare it for use.

By September 16, Hudson's crew had passed the Catskill Mountains and were around Albany. The crew bought Indian corn and pumpkins and filled their casks with fresh water. It was September 22 when the **scouts** who had traveled by boat about 25 miles (40 kilometers) farther reported that the ship could not continue because of the shallow depth of the river.

You can follow Hudson's voyage on the map on page 42.

New Yorkers are proud of Henry Hudson and have erected monuments to him and named a bridge and parkway after him.

The return trip

It was lucky that they did turn around. The next day they ran aground and were stuck for an hour until the tide lifted them up. Hudson reported: "The land is the finest for cultivation that I ever in my life set foot upon, and it also abounds in trees of every description. The natives are a very good people, for when they saw that I would not remain, they supposed that I was afraid of their bows, and taking the arrows, they broke them in pieces, and threw them into the fire."

Hudson had been entertained in a house made of well-constructed oak bark. He was seated on a mat and served food in red wooden bowls. Hunters were sent out for food and brought back a pair of pigeons. Also a fat dog was killed and skinned, using sharp shells.

Hudson was impressed with the beauty of the land near Albany, New York.

Juet reports that they came to a part of the river called Manna-hata. He thought that there must be a copper or silver mine there because of the white-green color of the cliff.

On October 4, 1609, the ship left the river and crossed the ocean, reaching England on November 7. Hudson's second-in-command, who was Dutch, had suggested that they spend the winter in Newfoundland and continue their search the next year, but Hudson rejected the idea because he thought that the cold climate might have caused another **mutiny.**

Choice of the crew

The English refused to let Hudson travel to Amsterdam to give his report on his third trip to the VOC, so Hudson gave his report to the Dutch **consul** in London. His fourth and last voyage was backed by an independent group of London merchants, who authorized him to search for the Northwest Passage. The English gave Hudson a larger ship, the *Discovery,* which carried a crew of 22. Five of the crew had sailed with Hudson before, including Robert Juet, who most likely was among the **mutineers** on the second voyage.

Before Hudson left England, he made two changes in the ship's personnel. He sent ashore Master Coleburne, who had signed on as an "adviser" to the merchants backing the expedition. Having an "adviser" aboard must have been irritating to Hudson. He added Henry Greene, a man with a shady reputation. Hudson probably knew about Greene's reputation, because he did not sign him on until after the sponsoring merchants had made their formal visit. Greene's name did not appear on any official crew list.

YOU CAN FOLLOW HUDSON'S VOYAGE ON THE MAP ON PAGE 43.

Robert Juet said to another crew member that Greene was acting as an "informer" to gain the confidence of crew members and then to provide evidence against any whom Hudson did not like. Hudson reacted so strongly to this accusation that he considered turning the ship around to put Juet off at Iceland.

The difficulties of the search for the Northwest Passage are illustrated by this woodcut of an 1850 expedition in which the ship was trapped in ice.

Hardships

Very few of the pages of Hudson's journal remain. However, historians have found an account of the voyage in a journal by a crew member, Abacuck Prickett, and a note discovered in the desk of another member of the crew.

The *Discovery* left on April 17, 1610 to search for a passage north of the places Hudson had explored on his third expedition. Therefore, he headed for Iceland and Greenland and over to the Davis **Strait.** He had to fight to keep the ship from being locked into a dense ice pack or destroyed by huge icebergs. It was at this point that Hudson brought out his chart, showed it to the crew, and then left it up to them whether or not to continue. They decided to continue, but it must have been clear that Hudson was not confident of his course.

They arrived in James Bay, where Hudson sailed back and forth looking for a westward passage in a way that seemed purposeless to others. Hudson decided to spend the winter at the southernmost part of James Bay. The crew hauled the ship onto land and built temporary shelters. That winter, lack of food, severe cold, and a lack of sunlight made the men sick.

On June 18, 1611, the ship was set afloat, but it soon was locked into ice with only fourteen days of skimpy food rations left. At this point, Hudson seemed to lose hope of ever finding an Arctic passage.

Hundreds of years after Hudson sailed, Arctic ice was still a problem for ships. In 1837, the British ship HMS Terror *was trapped in pack ice for 19 months. Few of the men survived.*

Mutiny

Cut adrift

The crew had just spent a miserable winter, and there didn't seem to be any hope of finding the passage they were looking for. Also, in the eyes of some of the men aboard, Hudson favored Henry Greene over other crew members. Then when Greene proved to be a problem by siding with people out of favor with Hudson, he turned against him. Juet and Greene banded together and convinced some other members of the crew to help them overthrow Hudson's command. **Mutiny** was punished in those days with death by hanging, so some men aboard tried to avoid any involvement.

On June 22, 1611, the leaders of the mutiny tied up Henry Hudson and put him, his son, and the sick men into the **shallop.** Philip Staffe, the ship's carpenter and Hudson's friend, chose to go with him rather than stay with the ship. Nine men were put in the boat, along with a gun, some spears, an iron pot, and some grain. They were towed out of some of the worst of the ice and cut adrift from the ship, which sailed east.

You can follow Hudson's voyage on the map on page 43.

The cold, lack of food, and a sense of mistrust led to the crew's revolt aboard the Discovery.

With limited food and supplies, Hudson and the eight other men did not stand much of a chance against the harsh weather.

The fate of the *Discovery*

After the mutiny it was doubtful that anyone left aboard the *Discovery* could get the ship home. Even with nine men gone, the food supply on the ship was very low. One of the passengers was put in charge of rationing the food that was left. Robert Bylot, one of the officers, became captain.

On July 28, the remaining crew met some Indians with whom they attempted to trade. Six of the men took a boat to the shore. The Indians attacked. Three of the men from the ship were killed, including Henry Greene. Two were wounded and later died.

The remaining men had to operate the boat and go ashore elsewhere to kill enough birds so that there would be food for the men during the crossing of the ocean. By the end of the voyage, the survivors had to eat candle wax and bird bones. The grain was gone. Robert Juet died when they were a short distance from Ireland. Of the thirteen men who stayed with the ship, only seven made it back to England.

What happened to Henry Hudson?

While much of Hudson's journal was destroyed by the **mutineers,** his map was not. It continued to excite others in a search for a northwest passage. In May of 1613, two ships—the *Resolution* and Hudson's own *Discovery*—were sent out to look for the passage, with Thomas Button as captain. Two crew members from Hudson's 1610 trip, Abacuck Prickett and Robert Bylot, were on board. They were confident that a northwest passage to the Pacific Ocean was possible. The voyage was also intended to look for Hudson and his men. Five men from this voyage were killed, and the ships returned to England after spending the winter on the western shore of Hudson Bay. The expedition proved that instead of reaching the Pacific Ocean, there was a western boundary to Hudson Bay.

In 1616, the *Discovery* returned after sailing 300 miles (480 kilometers) farther north. Robert Bylot, its captain, concluded that there was no hope of finding a passage. There was also no hope that Hudson would be found alive.

Other sea captains and Hudson Bay traders reported finding some stakes that had been sharpened with a European ax and the remains of a house on Danby Island. Had this been the work of Hudson's carpenter? No other sign of the men in the **shallop** was ever found.

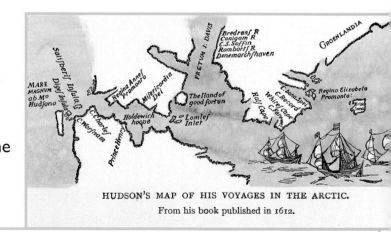

HUDSON'S MAP OF HIS VOYAGES IN THE ARCTIC.
From his book published in 1612.

The map of Hudson Bay drawn by Henry Hudson survived the mutiny and was sent to Hudson's friend in Holland. It was published and sold five editions in one year. The map corrected many errors on previous maps, but still encouraged the idea that Hudson Bay was the Northwest Passage.

The mutineers

When Robert Bylot and Abacuck Prickett returned to London and made their report to the merchants who had sponsored the 1610–1611 voyage, an immediate inquiry into the **mutiny** was not made. A month later a preliminary report declared that the mutineers deserved to be hanged. However, with the exception of the ship's surgeon, Edward Wilson, who gave his testimony in 1611, they were not even brought before the court until years later to give testimony.

Together with its southernmost part, James Bay, Hudson Bay is 1,050 miles (1,690 kilometers) long.

The survivors all blamed those who had died for the mutiny. They said that they had been in danger of starving to death, and that no one was hurt or shot at in the action. Since the ship had plenty of bloodstains that the rain and waves had not washed away on the journey home, this claim may be doubted. Bylot received a pardon for bringing the survivors home safely. The others either had the charges dismissed or were found not guilty in 1618. Perhaps the English, who were still interested in pursuing the Northwest Passage and gaining territory and trade in the New World, wanted to be able to use the talents of these men in future expeditions.

Hudson's Legacy

Success or failure?

Henry Hudson failed to find his northern route to Asia. He discovered no new continent. He may even have failed as the master of his ship. So why is he honored in the way that he is—with a bay, a river, a bridge, and many statues and monuments named after him?

What he accomplished in mapping out unknown territory is remarkable. He was not sailing on easy voyages, but under the most difficult conditions of snow, ice, storms, currents, and even unknown land masses. He was in constant danger of being caught and frozen in ice **floes** or being crushed by huge icebergs. He had to spend a winter in a land without much food or sunlight. His explorations contributed much knowledge, even though it was the news that there was no easy Arctic passage to Asia.

By providing the Dutch, who supported him, with a claim on the land he explored around the Hudson River, in what is now New York, he opened the way for Dutch colonists to settle in the land that later became the United States. He is now recognized as a bond between the Netherlands and the United States.

The Hudson Bridge in New York honors Henry Hudson's early efforts to open the New World to the Dutch.

Hero of the United States

While Hudson is deserving of world fame, he is specially honored in New York for his 1609 explorations with his ship, the *Half Moon*. In 1909, the citizens of Amsterdam built a replica of the ship for the Hudson-Fulton Celebration. The ship could have sailed from Amsterdam but was carried as cargo to New York by a ship of the Holland America Line. In New York it took part in ceremonies and sailed in New York Harbor and the Hudson River. However, interest in the ship did not continue. She was hauled up on land and accidentally destroyed by fire in 1934.

The 1989 replica of the Half Moon *has been put to good use touring ports and providing a training ship for the Sea Cadets.*

Then in 1989, a new replica of the *Half Moon* was built for the celebration of the New Netherland Festival in honor of the Dutch contributions to American life. Greater knowledge of the construction of the original ship resulted in a more accurate design for the ship, although modern construction materials were used. The ship is now the home of Sea Cadets. These are middle or high school students who come aboard for a week to learn how to sail such a ship under the direction of a licensed Coast Guard captain.

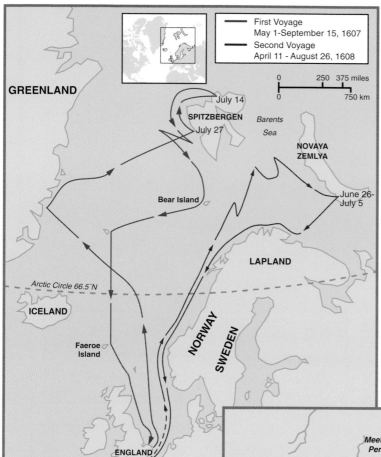

First Voyage
May 1-September 15, 1607

Second Voyage
April 11 - August 26, 1608

GREENLAND

July 14

SPITZBERGEN
July 27

Barents
Sea

NOVAYA
ZEMLYA

June 26-
July 5

Bear Island

LAPLAND

Arctic Circle 66.5˚N

ICELAND

Faeroe
Island

NORWAY

SWEDEN

ENGLAND

0   250   375 miles
0   750 km

Henry Hudson's first and second voyages were in search of a northeast passage to Asia. Both times he was turned back by ice.

Hudson's third voyage began with a brief exploration of the White Sea. He was stopped by ice and bad weather, but instead of going back to the Netherlands, as his contract demanded, the *Half Moon* sailed across the Atlantic. Hudson hoped to find an Arctic trade route above North America.

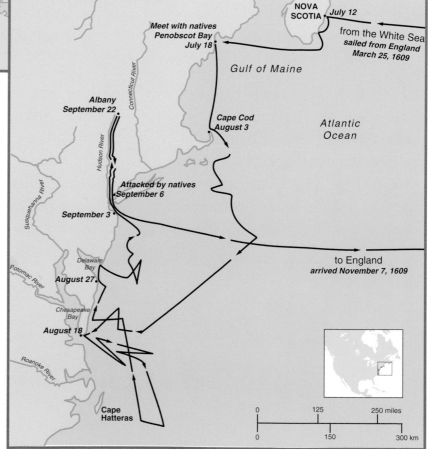

NOVA
SCOTIA   July 12

from the White Sea
*sailed from England
March 25, 1609*

Meet with natives
Penobscot Bay
July 18

Gulf of Maine

Connecticut River

Albany
September 22

Cape Cod
August 3

Atlantic
Ocean

Hudson River

Attacked by natives
September 6

September 3

Susquehanna River

Delaware
Bay

August 27

Potomac River

Chesapeake
Bay

August 18

to England
arrived November 7, 1609

Roanoke River

Cape
Hatteras

0   125   250 miles
0   150   300 km

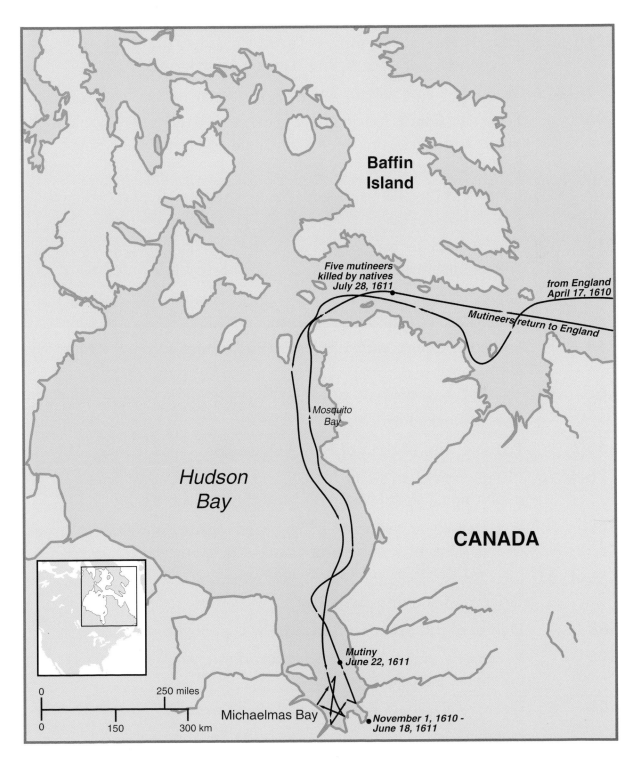

Baffin
Island

Five mutineers
killed by natives
July 28, 1611

from England
April 17, 1610

Mutineers return to England

Mosquito
Bay

Hudson
Bay

CANADA

Mutiny
June 22, 1611

0   250 miles

0   150   300 km

Michaelmas Bay

November 1, 1610 -
June 18, 1611

Hudson's final voyage ended in **mutiny.** Seven of the **mutineers** returned safely to England, but Hudson was never heard from again.

Timeline

1492–1493	First voyage of Christopher Columbus to the New World
1497	John Cabot, looking for a northwest passage, discovers Newfoundland, Canada, and claims it for England
1497–1499	Vasco da Gama sails around Africa to India
1508	Sebastian Cabot, looking for a northwest passage, finds a land mass stretching from the Arctic Circle to North Carolina or perhaps even Florida
1519–1522	Ferdinand Magellan, sailing for Spain, becomes the first to circle the globe
1524	Giovanni da Verrazano, sailing for the French, explores from somewhere south of North Carolina up to the Arctic
1534–1541	Jaques Cartier makes three voyages for France, exploring the Gulf of St. Lawrence
1548	Sebastian Cabot, with 100 English merchants, forms the Muscovy Company
1556	The Muscovy Company's attempt to find a northeast passage to Asia is blocked by ice
1565(?)	Possible date of birth of Henry Hudson
1576–1578	Martin Frobisher, sailing for England, makes three voyages exploring Labrador, Baffin Bay, and the Hudson **Straits**
1585	In a meeting at the home of Thomas Hudson, John Davis plans a trip to hunt for a northwest passage from England to Asia
1585–1587	John Davis, sailing for England, makes three voyages exploring Greenland and into Baffin Bay
1588	Defeat of the **Spanish Armada** by the English navy
1596	Willem Barent, a Dutch **navigator,** dies trying to find a northeast passage
1603	Death of Elizabeth I of England; James I becomes king
1607	Hudson's first voyage reaches as far as Spitzbergen
1608	Hudson's second voyage takes him as far as Siberia and Russia

1609	Hudson's third voyage reaches as far south as the Carolinas
1610–11	Hudson's fourth voyage ends in **mutiny**
1611	Possible date of death of Henry Hudson
1613	Two English ships are sent to find a northwest passage and to look for Henry Hudson and his men
1616	The *Discovery,* with Robert Bylot as captain and William Baffin as pilot, explores farther north and concludes that there is no hope Hudson survived, and no hope of finding an ice-free passage
1618	**Mutineers** from Hudson's last voyage are either found not guilty, or the charges against them are dropped
1969	First commercial vessel makes its way through the Northwest Passage from Alaska to New York

More Books to Read

Goodman, Joan E. *Beyond the Sea of Ice: The Voyages of Henry Hudson.* New York: Mikaya Press, 1999.

Morley, Jacqueline. *Exploring North America.* Lincolnwood, Ill.: NTC Contemporary Publishing Co., 1996.

Whitcraft, Melissa. *The Hudson River.* Danbury, Conn.: Franklin Watts, Inc., 1999.

Wilbur, Keith C. *Early Explorers of North America.* Broomall, Penn.: Chelsea House Publishers, 1996.

Young, Karen Romano. *Arctic Investigations: Exploring the Frozen Ocean.* Austin, Tex.: Raintree Steck-Vaughn Publishers, 1999.

Glossary

blubber fat from sea animals, such as whales, that can be made into oil

calve to separate from a glacier, like an iceberg

cask large wooden container used for storing liquids

certificate official document that serves as proof of some fact

chronometer device for measuring time

colony group of people sent out by a state to settle a new territory

communion religious ceremony commemorating the last supper of Jesus

conquistador leader in the Spanish conquest of the Americas during the fifteenth and sixteenth centuries

consul government official who lives in another country to help his or her fellow citizens who are also in that country

empire group of territories or peoples under one ruler

floe sheet or mass of floating ice

florin type of coin used in the Netherlands

guilder another type of coin used in the Netherlands

latitude distance north or south from the equator

longitude distance east or west, measured from the prime meridian

mast long pole that rises from the bottom of a ship and supports the sails

mermaid imaginary sea creature having the upper body of a woman but the tail of a fish

musket type of old-fashioned gun, similar to a rifle, that is loaded through the muzzle

Muslim believer in Islam, a religion based on belief in Allah, started by the prophet Muhammad

mutineer person who takes part in a mutiny

mutiny to refuse, as a group, to obey authority

navigator officer on a ship responsible for figuring out its position and course

outfit to equip for a voyage

pope leader of the Roman Catholic Church

Reformation European religious movement of the sixteenth century in which Protestant churches split from the Roman Catholic Church

rig shape, number, and arrangement of sails

scout to explore an area to obtain information, or someone who goes on such a mission

shallop small, open boat fitted with oars or sails, or both

Silk Road trade route that stretched from China to the Mediterranean

Spanish Armada fleet of ships sent by Spain to attack England in 1588 that was defeated

spar long, rounded piece of wood to which a sail is fastened

stern rear end of a boat

strait narrow channel connecting two bodies of water

suckle to feed from the breast or udder

terrain piece of land

uncharted not yet explored or mapped

Index

Africa 7, 8, 12
Alaska 7
Albany, New York 32
Amsterdam 20, 23
Arkhangelsk, Russia 13
Arctic 4, 7, 10, 12, 18, 24
Asia 4-7, 10, 12, 20, 40

Baffin Bay 10
Baffin Island 7
Baffin, William 38
Barrent, Willem 17
Bylot, Robert 37-39

Cabot, John 10
Cabot, Sebastian 10, 13
Canada (See Hudson Bay,
   Newfoundland) 5, 7, 10, 12, 28
Cape Cod 29
Cape Hatteras 29
Cape of Good Hope 8
Cape Sable 26
Cartier, Jacques 10, 18
Catskill Mountains 32
Chesapeake Bay 5
China 6, 14, 28, 29
Colman, John 31
Columbus, Christopher 8, 20
Cortés, Hernàn 8
Croton-on-Hudson, New York
   23, 41

Danby Island 38
Davis, John 4, 10, 35
Davis Strait 35
Discovery, The 34-39
Dutch East India Company (VOC)
   20-23, 5, 34

East Indies 6
Elizabeth I 9
England 5-7, 9, 10, 12-14, 20, 23,
   25, 29, 33, 34, 37

Florida 10
France 10, 20, 26, 27
Frobisher, Martin 26

Gama, Vasco da 8
George's Harbor 27
Great Lakes 28
Greene, Henry 34, 36, 37
Greenland 5, 10, 14, 35
Gulf of Maine 26

Gulf of St. Lawrence 10
Gulf Stream 29

Half Moon 5, 22-33, 40, 41
Holland (See Netherlands, the)
Hope-well 14, 15
Hudson Bay 5, 35-39
Hudson Bridge 40
Hudson, Henry 4, 5, 11, 13-21,
   23-38, 40, 41
Hudson, John 4, 14-17, 36, 37
Hudson, Katherine 4, 21
Hudson River 5, 28-33, 40, 41
Hudson Straits 5, 10
Hudson, Thomas 4

ice 10, 13, 15, 17, 34-37, 40
Iceland 34, 35
India 8, 23, 29
Indian Ocean 7
Indonesia 23

Jakarta, Indonesia 23
James Bay 35
James River (King's River) 28, 29
Japan 14
Juet, Robert 22, 24, 26, 27, 29-31,
   34-36

Kara Sea 12, 16

latitude 11
London 14, 19, 25
longitude 11

Magdalena Bay 15
Magellan, Ferdinand 8
Maine 5, 26, 27
Manhattan, the 7
Manna-hata 33
Massachusetts 27, 29
mermaid 19
Moscow 13
Muscovy Adventurers 13
Muscovy Company 4, 13, 16, 18,
   20, 25

Native Americans 27, 30-33, 37
Netherlands, the 5-7, 9, 20, 21,
   23-25, 29, 34, 40
New York 10, 23, 29-33, 40, 41
Newfoundland 10, 26, 55
North Cape 24
North Carolina 5, 10
North Pole 12, 14

Northeast Passage 12, 16-19, 21,
   24
Northwest Passage 4, 5, 7, 10,
   12, 21, 24, 34, 38, 39
Norway 24
Nova Scotia 5, 26
Novaya Zemlya 16, 17, 18, 21

Ob River 16

pope 8, 9
Portugal 7, 8, 10, 12
Prickett, Abacuck 35, 38, 39

Reformation 9
Russia 5, 12, 13

St. George River 27
St. Lawrence River 28
Scandinavia 5
Sea of Verrazano 29
Siberia 5, 16
Silk Road 6
Smith, Captain John 28, 29
South America 12
South Carolina 5, 29
Spain 8, 9, 10, 12, 13
Spanish Armada 9
Spitzbergen 5, 14, 15, 17
Staffe, Philip 36, 38
Staten Island 29

Tisquantum 27

United States 23, 40, 41

Verrazano, Giovanni da 10, 29
Vikings 11
Virginia 28, 29
VOC (See Dutch East India
   Company)

West Indies 10
White Sea 13, 24
Wilson, Edward 39